LOOKING AT COUNTRIES

Looking at
INDIA

Jillian Powell

GS
PUBLISHING
A Member of the WRC Media Family of Companies

Please visit our web site at: www.garethstevens.com
For a free color catalog describing Gareth Stevens Publishing's list
of high-quality books and multimedia programs, call 1-800-542-2595 (USA)
or 1-800-387-3178 (Canada). Gareth Stevens Publishing's fax: (414) 332-3567.

Library of Congress Cataloging-in-Publication Data

Powell, Jillian.
    Looking at India / Jillian Powell.
        p. cm. — (Looking at countries)
    Includes index.
    ISBN-13: 978-0-8368-7669-7 (lib. bdg.)
    ISBN-13: 978-0-8368-7676-5 (softcover)
    1. India—Juvenile literature. I. Title.
    DS407.P65   2006
    954—dc22   2006034463

4339   4757   04/10

This North American edition first published in 2007 by
Gareth Stevens Publishing
A Member of the WRC Media Family of Companies
330 West Olive Street, Suite 100
Milwaukee, Wisconsin 53212 USA

This U.S. edition copyright © 2007 by Gareth Stevens, Inc.
Original edition copyright © 2006 by Franklin Watts.
First published in Great Britain in 2006 by Franklin Watts,
338 Euston Road, London NW1 3BH, United Kingdom.

Series editor: Sarah Peutrill
Art director: Jonathan Hair
Design: Rita Storey
Picture research: Diana Morris

Gareth Stevens editor: Dorothy L. Gibbs
Gareth Stevens art direction: Tammy West
Gareth Stevens graphic designer: Charlie Dahl

Photo credits: (t=top, b=bottom, l=left, r=right, c=center)
Dinodia Photo Library: all photos, except the following. Binder/Superbild/A1 pix: 27t.
Superbild/A1 Pix: front cover, 11, 20, 26.

Every effort has been made to trace the copyright holders for the photos used in this book. The publisher apologizes,
in advance, for any unintentional omissions and would be pleased to insert the appropriate acknowledgements in any
subsequent edition of this publication.

Printed in Canada

1 2 3 4 5 6 7 8 9 10 10 09 08 07 06

Contents

Words that appear in the glossary are printed in **boldface** type the first time they occur in the text.

Where is India?

India is a large country in Asia. It is the seventh largest country in the world.

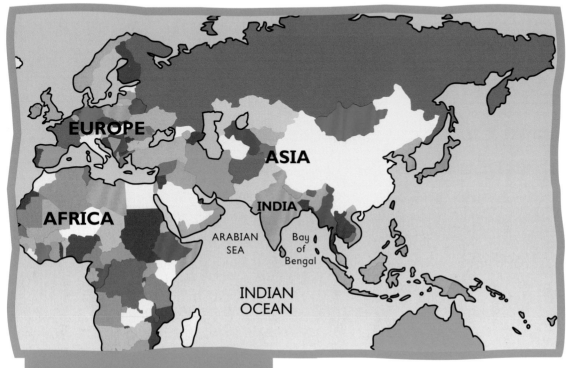

The southern part of India is a **peninsula** that reaches into the Indian Ocean.

India's capital city is New Delhi. It is in the northern part of the country. New Delhi is an important business center, with banks, offices, factories, shops, and an international airport.

These large buildings in **New Delhi** have government offices inside.

4

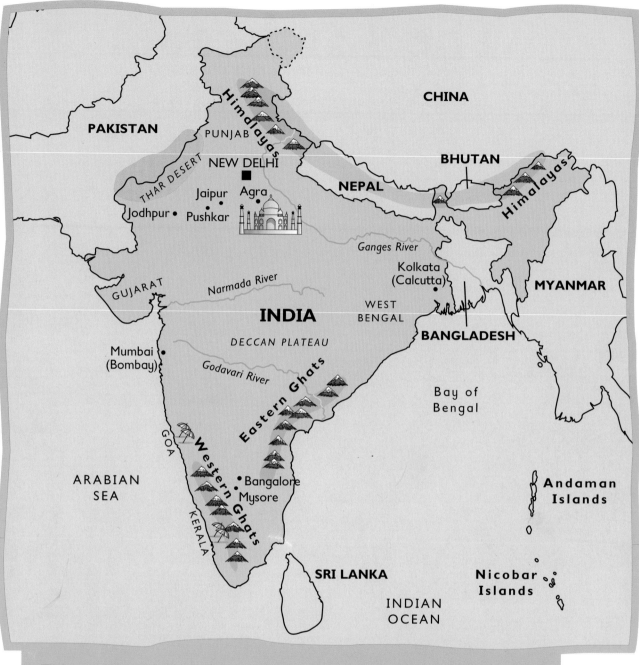

This map shows all the places that are mentioned in this book.

India has a long coastline, with the Arabian Sea to the west, the Bay of Bengal to the east, and the Indian Ocean to the south.

Did you know?

People in India call their country Bharat (bah ROT).

The Landscape

Different parts of India have very different landscapes. In the north, the Himalaya Mountains have some of the highest peaks in the world. West of the Himalayas, the dry Thar Desert crosses India's northwest border into Pakistan.

The tops of the high Himalayas are covered with snow all year round.

The middle of the country is a large area of low, flat land. Three great rivers, including the Ganges, cross this huge central plain. Most of India's people live in this region and work on the **fertile** farmland there.

Did you know?

Tigers still live in the wild in India's jungles.

Fields of mustard plants are common in Punjab. This Indian state is in a dry region between the Thar Desert and the Himalaya Mountains.

Further south, the Deccan Plateau is a large area of high, flat land. The forested mountains of the Eastern and Western Ghats lie along each side of the plateau.

Southern India also has beautiful sandy beaches, especially along the western coastline, in the states of Goa and Kerala.

Beaches like this one in Goa draw tourists to India from all over the world.

Weather and Seasons

India has three main seasons. The cool winter months last from October to February.

Summer follows, with hot, dry weather that causes **droughts** in many parts of the country until June. Then the **monsoon** season starts.

During droughts, people, like these women in Gujarat, often have to collect water in containers from any place they can find it.

The monsoon season in India means heavy rains every day.

During the monsoon season, warm winds blow in from the Indian Ocean, bringing heavy rains and flooding. Some monsoon storms, called cyclones, are fierce. These storms have very high winds that sometimes cause **tidal waves** along India's eastern coastline.

The coolest temperatures in India are in the Himalaya mountains. The hottest temperatures are in the Thar Desert, where high temperatures can reach 115 °Fahrenheit (45 °Celsius) in summer heat.

Did you know?

Many Indian songs and poems celebrate the arrival of monsoon rains.

Indian People

More than one billion people live in India. More people live in this country than in any other country of the world, except China. Each state in India has its own language, clothing styles, and **traditions**.

Religion is important to the people of India. They say prayers every day and follow the rules of their religions. Most Indian people are Hindus, but some are Muslims, Sikhs, or Christians.

Most Hindu homes have shrines, where families say their daily prayers.

A street market in the town of Pushkar is a busy place. Besides speaking Hindi and English, the people of Pushkar speak Rajasthani and Gujarati.

Hindi is India's main language, but there are eighteen other state languages and more than 1,600 different **dialects**. The English language is used in India for business and government. In India's schools, children usually learn Hindi, English, and their state languages.

School and Family

Children in India start school when they are six or seven years old. Schooling is free for all children up to age fourteen.

Even with free schooling, however, many children from poor families do not go to school or go for only a few years. These children have to work to help bring in money for their families. India's poorest children live on the streets and beg for money.

The children at this school in West Bengal line up in class groups each morning before their lessons start.

Family celebrations are common in most Indian homes.

Family life is very important in India. Children, parents, and grandparents often live together in the same house. Indian relatives almost always get together to celebrate family events and religious festivals.

Country Life

Most people in India live in the countryside. Many of them farm small plots of land to grow food for their families. Some country families also raise cows for milk.

Most of the work on family farms, such as planting and harvesting crops, is done by hand. Oxen or water buffalo are sometimes used to pull farm carts. Children help with farm work and daily household tasks, such as **fetching** water from village wells.

This young boy is cooling off with water taken from a village well.

Did you know?

In India, people sometimes paint the horns on their cows to show which family owns the cows.

Street sellers use bicycles to carry the goods they want to sell from village to village.

To bring in a little money, some people grow extra crops on their land and sell or trade them at markets. Others weave cloth or baskets or make other crafts to sell at markets.

City Life

India's cities have grown fast. Many young people have moved away from the countryside to find work in the cities.

New Delhi, the capital of India, is a crowded city, with many businesses and government buildings. Bangalore is a city of high-tech companies and research centers. Mumbai, which is India's largest city and seaport, is a center for trade and industry.

Did you know?

The city of Mumbai used to be known as Bombay.

This street in New Delhi is ready for a festival.

16

City streets in India, such as this street in Mumbai, are full of traffic.

All of India's cities share problems of overcrowding, **poverty**, and **pollution**. The roads are packed with cars, trucks, buses, streetcars, motorbikes, and **bicycle rickshaws**.

While rich people in the cities enjoy a modern lifestyle, with shopping, restaurants, health clubs and nightlife, many people live in poverty, without jobs, homes, or health care.

Indian Houses

Many people in India's cities live in modern apartment buildings. The richest people have big houses with modern conveniences such as air-conditioning and satellite television.

Did you know?

Jodhpur is called the Blue City because many of its houses are painted blue.

This brightly painted house in Mumbai is a fisherman's home.

These modern buildings in Jaipur are apartment houses.

These traditional village houses in the state of Gujarat are made of mud and straw and have **palm thatch** roofs.

Traditional village houses in India are often built around a courtyard that has a shrine for daily prayer. These houses usually have one big room, where the family lives, along with a storeroom and a shelter for the animals.

Indian Food

Most Indian food is colorful and spicy. People like to shop for fresh foods and spices from local markets.

Meatless dishes, such as spicy vegetable stews and sweet milk puddings made with nuts and spices, are popular in India. Hindu Indians eat no meat. Muslims eat no pork.

Bowls of colorful spices brighten this market stall in Mysore.

Did you know?

The dish called Bombay duck is really fried fish!

In southern India, stews are eaten with rice or served with rice cakes or rice-flour pancakes. In northern India, many dishes are served with flat breads, such as *parathas* or *chapatis*.

This woman is cooking chapatis outdoors. This kind of flat bread is thin, like a pancake.

At mealtimes, Indian families like to eat together. They share several dishes with foods such as rice, spicy vegetables, and yogurt.

At home, Indians often eat meals sitting cross-legged on the floor.

At Work

Industries in India include farming, fishing, **textiles**, machinery, chemicals, aircraft, cars, and computers. The tourist industry brings millions of visitors from all over the world to India's bustling cities, beautiful beaches, and famous buildings, such as the Taj Mahal.

Building cars and other kinds of machines are growing industries in India.

Did you know?

Bangalore is known as Asia's Silicon City because of its fast-growing technology industry.

Workers in a call center are talking on telephones all day long.

Service industries in the cities, such as banks, travel agencies, cell phone companies, and **call centers** are providing more jobs for women workers in India.

In the countryside, most people work on farms, using only simple hand tools and water buffalo and oxen to help them. Millions of village children help out on farms. Children also make or sell goods to bring in a little money for their families.

A long stick is the only tool this farmer in the state of Gujarat uses to keep his herd of animals moving.

Having Fun

People in India's big cities like to go to movies. They especially enjoy watching Bollywood movies, which are made by Mumbai's film industry. At home, some of the richer families have satellite or cable television.

This Bollywood movie poster is advertising a comedy.

Throwing colored powder, called *gulal*, on each other is part of the fun when the people of India celebrate the spring festival of Holi.

India has many colorful religious festivals throughout the year. **Holi** and **Divali** are both Hindu festivals. The people of India celebrate these festivals by feasting, dressing up, dancing, and watching fireworks.

Many people in India enjoy sports. Field hockey, cricket, and soccer are some of the most popular sports, both to watch and to play. India also has some very popular traditional sports, including camel and elephant racing and team games such as *kabaddi*.

Field hockey is India's national sport.

25

India: The Facts

- India is the largest country in southern Asia.

- It is a **republic** and a member of the **Commonwealth of Nations**. The President is the **head of state**, and the Prime Minister leads the government.

- India is made up of twenty-eight states and seven territories. Each state and territory has its own government. India's territories include some of the larger cities as well as some islands, such as the Andaman and Nicobar Islands.

- India has the second largest population in the world. China is the only country with more people.

- India's main cities include New Delhi (the capital city), Mumbai (Bombay), Kolkata (Calcutta), and Bangalore.

The Indian flag has orange, white, and green bands, with a Buddhist symbol in the center of the white band. Green stands for rich land, white stands for peace, and orange stands for courage.

The Taj Mahal, in Agra, is one of India's most famous landmarks.

Did you know?

The Taj Mahal was built as a tomb for an Empress.

Indian currency is the rupee.

Glossary

bicycle rickshaws – small carts or wheeled vehicles that carry passengers and are pulled by people on bicycles

call center – a place where workers answer telephone calls for different types of businesses to help their customers

Commonwealth of Nations – a group of independent countries that were once ruled by Great Britain

dialects – local ways of speaking a language

Divali – the Hindu Festival of Lights, held in late October or early November

droughts – long periods of time without rain that are harmful to plants and animals in the area

fertile – having rich soil that is good for growing crops

fetching – going after something and bringing it back

head of state – the main representative of a country

Holi – a springtime celebration in northern India, often called the Festival of Color

kabaddi – a team game that combines a type of rugby or football and wrestling

monsoon – strong, warm winds that blow in from over an ocean and bring heavy rains onto land

palm thatch – palm tree branches that are bound together to make a thick, protective covering

peninsula – a strip of land that sticks out into a body of water and is surrounded by water on three sides

pollution – dirt in the air, on land, or in bodies of water that is caused by waste and chemicals from industries and traffic

poverty – the state or condition of being very, very poor

republic – a kind of government in which decisions are made by the people of the country and their representatives

shrines – small areas, often decorated with religious objects, which people use as special places to pray

textiles – threads, yarns, woven materials and cloths, or fabrics

tidal waves – huge ocean waves that crash onto coastlands, causing floods and other kinds of damage

traditions – the ways of living and beliefs of certain people that have been passed down through generations

Find Out More

Ancient India
www.historyforkids.org/learn/india/

Explore the Taj Mahal
www.taj-mahal.net

Time for Kids: India
www.timeforkids.com/TFK/hh/goplaces/main/
   0,20344,610558,00.html

Publisher's note to educators and parents: Our editors have carefully reviewed these Web sites to ensure that they are suitable for children. Many Web sites change frequently, however, and we cannot guarantee that a site's future contents will continue to meet our high standards of quality and educational value. Be advised that children should be closely supervised whenever they access the Internet.

My Map of India

Photocopy or trace the map on page 31. Then write in the names of the countries, bodies of water, island groups, land areas and mountains, states, and cities listed below. (Look at the map on page 5 if you need help.)

After you have written in the names of all the places, find some crayons and color the map!

Countries
China
India
Pakistan

Bodies of Water
Arabian Sea
Bay of Bengal
Ganges River
Indian Ocean

Island Groups
Andaman Islands
Nicobar Islands

Land Areas and Mountains
Deccan Plateau
Eastern Ghats
Himalayas
Thar Desert
Western Ghats

States
Goa
Gujarat
Kerala
Punjab
West Bengal

Cities
Agra
Bangalore
Jaipur
Jodhpur
Kolkata (Calcutta)
Mumbai (Bombay)
Mysore
New Delhi (capital)
Pushkar

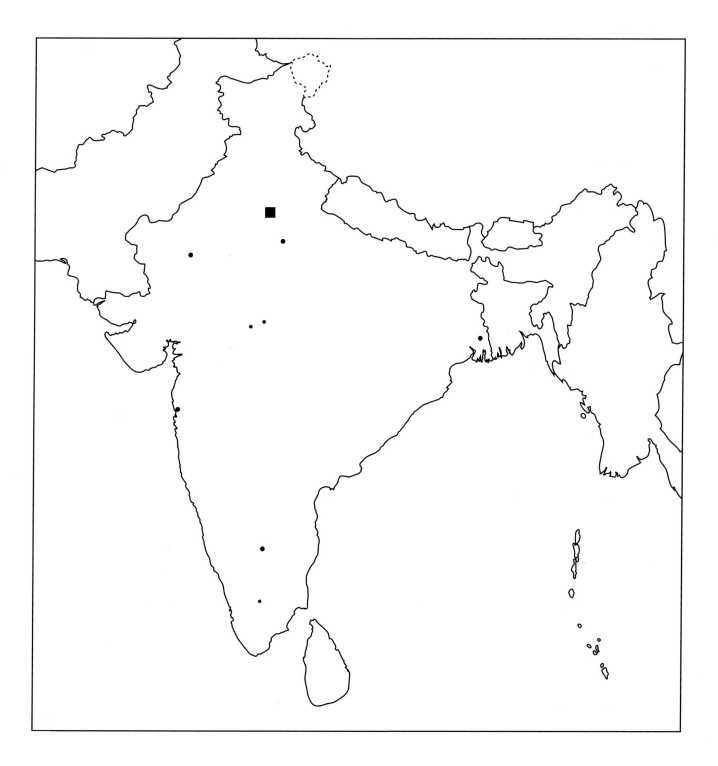

Index